Laced wit

To Margaret and Rob, for their contribution to the Australian craft industry. We have watched them learn, grow and prosper; a fine example to all of us who are willing to strive for achievement through honest hard work, long hours and very little thanks.

Vicki Moodie.

Copyright: R and V Moodie   1994

Revised: November 2000.

All rights reserved. Except as provided under the copyright act, no part of this book may be reproduced in any form or by any means, including photocopying, without permission in writing from the author.

ISBN 1 876373 40 7

Published by

CRAFT MOODS
P.O.Box 126
Wamuran Qld. 4512
Australia

Phone/Fax (07) 5496 6826
www.craftmoods.com.au

Printed By   JT-PRESS
17 High Street
Redcliffe Qld 4020

Phone (07) 3283 0100
Fax (07) 3284 1477

11/00

CONTENTS

Page

Abbreviations 2
General Instructions 3
Types of eyelet lace 4

PATTERNS:

  1. Knitted cushion 5
  2. Crocheted cushion 6
  3. Knitted tidy bin cover 9
  4. Knitted lampshade 10
  5. Crocheted lampshade 12
  6. Knitted compact tissue cover 14
  7. Knitted lady towel motif 15
  8. Knitted scrunchie 17
  9. Crocheted lady towel motif 18
10. Knitted plastic bag holder 20
11. Knitted double toilet roll holder 21
12. Knitted bootees 22
13. Crocheted bootees 24
14. Knitted tissue box cover 26
15. Knitted golf club cover 28
16. Crocheted tidy bag 29
17. Crocheted wire coat hanger cover 32
18. Knitted angel 33

ABBREVIATIONS

ch	chain	P	purl
dc	double crochet	sl st	slip stitch
htr	half treble	st(s)	stitch(es)
K	knit	tog	together
MC	main colour	tr	treble

GENERAL INSTRUCTIONS

HOW TO KNIT IN LACE
From the left, place lace to back of work, insert needle into the first stitch and through first eyelet hole in lace, yarn over needle and complete the stitch. Keep the tension loose. Follow this procedure to end of row and cut off lace only.

HOW TO SLIP STITCH IN LACE
From the left, place lace to back of work, insert hook under first stitch and through first eyelet hole in lace, yarn over hook, pull yarn through hole, the stitch and the loop on hook. Keep the tension loose. Follow this procedure to end of row and cut off lace only.

TO NEATEN END OF LACE ROWS
To neaten ends of lace rows, overlap lace towards you by one hole at beginning and end of row.

TO JOIN LACE
To join eyelet lace part way through a row, just overlap each piece of lace by two sets of holes.

TYPES OF EYELET LACE
The different types of eyelet lace used in these patterns are shown actual size on page 4. Unless otherwise stated, use double sided eyelet lace.

FANCY WIDE EYELET LACES
Because fancy wide laces vary in the number of holes per metre depending on the header lace, the number of holes required has been given with each pattern. Metreage required is determined by the number of holes given, divided by the number of holes per metre. Check this with your stockist.

TYPES OF EYELET LACE (actual size)

1. KNITTED CUSHION

MATERIALS:
110g acrylic 8ply yarn
6.4m each of 4 colours (C1 - C4) eyelet lace
40cm plain fabric
500g polyester fibre fill
3 press studs
pr 4mm knitting needles

This project is knitted in garter stitch.

Tension: 19sts to 10cm.

FRONT (Make 4 similar squares)

Cast on 32sts and knit 2 rows.

* Knit in a row of lace C1.

Knit 3 rows. *

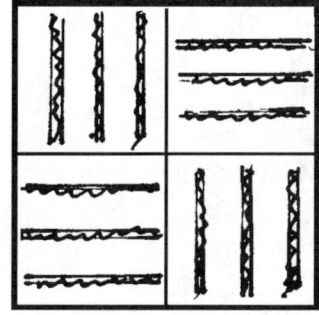

Repeat from * to * 15 more times working stripes by changing the colour of the lace to C2, C3, C4, C1, C2 etc. (16 rows of lace total)

Knit 2 rows. Cast off.

Right sides together, using backstitch, join squares as per diagram taking care not to catch in the lace.

BACK
Cast on 64sts, and knit 130 rows. Cast off loosely.

Make up: Place back and front right sides together. Sew together 3 sides and all except a 20cm central opening on the fourth side. Turn right side out. Sew press studs at opening. Make a fabric insert cushion using two 40cm squares of fabric. Sew together as for knitted cover. Stuff with fibre fill and sew opening closed. Place insert into knitted cover and fasten studs.

2. CROCHETED CUSHION

MATERIALS:
120g acrylic 8ply yarn main colour (MC)
35g each 2 contrast colours (C1 and C2) acrylic 8ply yarn
500g polyester fibre fill
10.5m eyelet lace
40cm plain fabric
3 press studs
3.5mm crochet hook

Tension: 17htr and 13 rows to 10cm.

FRONT
Using MC make 3ch.

Row 1. 2htr into 3rd ch from hook. (2htr, turning ch not counted as a stitch)

Row 2. 2ch, 2htr into first htr, 2htr into next htr. (4htr)

Row 3. 1ch, sl st in a row of lace *using every second hole.*

Row 4. 2ch, 2htr into first st, 1htr into each of the next 2sts, 2htr into the last st. (6htr)

Row 5. 2ch, 2htr into the first htr, 1htr into each of the next 4htr, 2htr into the last htr. (8htr)

Row 6. 2ch, 2htr into the first htr, 1htr into each of the next 6htr, 2htr into the last htr. (10htr)

Row 7. 1ch, sl st in a row of lace *using every second hole.*

Continue increasing 1htr at each end of row (as per rows 4 - 6) and slip stitching in lace every 4th row (as per row 7) until you have increased to 52sts and completed 9 rows of lace. (Middle row of cushion)

Row 36. 2ch, decrease over next 2sts, 1htr into each of the next 48sts, decrease over the last 2sts. (50htr)

Row 37. 2ch, decrease over next 2sts, 1htr into each of the next 46sts, decrease over the last 2sts. (48htr)

Row 38. 2ch, decrease over next 2sts, 1htr into each of the next 44sts, decrease over the last 2sts. (46htr)

Row 39. 1ch, sl st in a row of lace *using every second hole.*

Continue decreasing 1htr at each end of row (as per rows 36 - 38) and slip stitching in lace every 4th row (as per row 39) until you have decreased to 4sts and completed 17 rows of lace. (4sts)

Row 68. 2ch, (decrease over the next 2sts) twice. (2htr)

Row 69. 2ch, 1htr into each htr. (2htr) End off.

Using MC, pick up 38sts evenly along any one of the four edges.

Row 1. 2ch, 1htr into each st. (38htr)

Row 2. 2ch, decrease over next 2sts, 1htr into each of the next 34htr, decrease over last 2htr. (36htr)

Row 3. 2ch, decrease over next 2sts, 1htr into each of the next 32htr, decrease over last 2htr. (34htr)

Join in C1. Continue decreasing in the same manner working 3 rows. (28htr)

Join in C2. Continue decreasing in the same manner working 3 rows. (22htr)

Join in MC. Continue decreasing in the same manner working 3 rows. (16htr)

Join in C1. Continue decreasing in the same manner working 3 rows. (10htr)

Join in C2. Continue decreasing in the same manner working 3 rows. (4htr)

Row 19. 2ch, (decrease over the next 2htr) twice. (2htr)

End off.

Repeat for the other three edges.

Refer to diagram and join corners by working 2 rows of dc around edge, having 58dc on each side of cushion.

BACK

Make 58ch.

Row 1. 2ch, 1htr into each st. (58htr)

Repeat 52 times. End off.

Make up:

Place back and front right sides together. Sew together 3 sides and all except a 20cm central opening on the fourth side. Turn right side out. * Sew press studs at opening. Make 4 tassels and attach to corners.

Make a fabric insert cushion using two 40cm squares of fabric. Sew together as for crocheted cover to *. Stuff with fibre fill and sew opening closed. Place insert into crocheted cover and fasten studs.

3. KNITTED TIDY BIN COVER

MATERIALS:
40g 8ply acrylic yarn
3.8m (495 holes) of 3.5cm wide single sided gathered eyelet lace (130 holes/m)
large juice tin (49cm circumference 18cm high)
1m of 6mm wide ribbon
folk art paint (optional)
pr 4mm knitting needles

This project is knitted in garter stitch.

Tension: 16sts to 10cm, over knitting when lace knitted in.

Cast on 77sts.

Knit 14 rows.

* Knit in a row of lace.

Knit 11 rows. *

Repeat from * to * 4 more times.

Knit in a row of lace. (6 lace rows total)

Cast off loosely.

Make up:
If desired, paint the tin with folk art paint. A disposable liner can be fitted to the tin, being held in place by the knitted cover. Right sides together, join the back seam, taking care not to catch in the lace. Turn right side out. Neaten the turned under lace edges at back seam. Beginning at centre front, thread the ribbon through the lace holes at the top, pull up to fit tin and tie in a bow.

4. KNITTED LAMPSHADE

MATERIALS:
55g 4ply cotton
8.1m (1044 holes) of 5cm wide single sided gathered eyelet lace (130 holes/m)
30cm tiffany scalloped lampshade frame
flowers
1.5m of 10mm wide ribbon
pr 4mm knitting needles

This project is worked in garter stitch and knitted on oversized needles to achieve loose work and enable stretching over lampshade frame.

Tension: 22sts to 10cm.

To neaten ends of lace rows, overlap lace towards you by one hole at beginning of row. At end of row cut off lace without folding.

Cast on 168sts and knit 7 rows.

Row 8. Knit in a row of lace.

Knit 6 rows.

Row 15. * K12, K2 tog; repeat from * 11 more times. (156sts)

Row 16. Knit in a row of lace.

Knit 6 rows.

Row 23. * K11, K2 tog; repeat from * 11 more times. (144sts)

Row 24. Knit in a row of lace.

Knit 6 rows.

Row 31. * K10, K2 tog; repeat from * 11 more times. (132sts)

Row 32. Knit in a row of lace.

Knit 6 rows.

Row 39. * K9, K2 tog; repeat from * 11 more times. (120sts)

Row 40. Knit in a row of lace.

Knit 6 rows.

Row 47. * K8, K2 tog; repeat from * 11 more times. (108sts)

Row 48. Knit in a row of lace.

Knit 6 rows.

Row 55. * K7, K2 tog; repeat from * 11 more times. (96sts)

Row 56. Knit in a row of lace.

Knit 6 rows.

Row 63. * K6, K2 tog; repeat from * 11 more times. (84sts)

Row 64. Knit in a row of lace. (8 rows of lace completed)

Knit 1 row.

Row 66. * K5, K2 tog; repeat from * 11 more times. (72sts)

Work 2 rows. Cast off loosely.

Make up: Right sides together, sew side seam taking care not to catch in the lace. Neaten edges of lace. Place over wire frame, aligning the seam over one strut. Evenly oversew top and bottom edges over the wire frame. Make 3 bows from ribbon and sew to cover. Glue flowers to bows.

5. CROCHETED LAMPSHADE

MATERIALS:
50g 4ply cotton
5.9m (765 holes) of 3.5cm wide single sided gathered eyelet lace (130 holes/m)
25cm tiffany plain lampshade
flowers
1.5m of 10mm wide ribbon
3mm crochet hook

Note that this project is worked loosely so that the cover may be stretched over the lampshade frame.

Tension: 16tr to 10cm and 10 rows to 10cm.

Make 132ch. Join with a sl st to form a circle, ensuring the chains are not twisted.

Round 1. 2ch, 1tr into each st, sl st into the top of the 2ch. (132tr. Note the 2ch counts as 1tr)

Round 2. (Right side of work) 2ch, 1tr into each tr, sl st into the top of the 2ch. (132tr)

Round 3. Sl st across one more tr, turn work, (wrong side of work facing) 1ch, sl st in a row of lace, overlapping last 2 holes of lace and turning under lace to neaten edge at last st. Turn work.

Round 4. With right side of work facing, 1dc and 1ch in first st, 1tr in each stitch to end, sl st into the top of the first ch.

Round 5. 2ch in first st, 1tr into each of the next 8tr, decrease over next 2tr, * 1tr into each of the next 9tr, decrease over the next 2tr; repeat from * 10 more times, sl st into the top of the 2ch. (120tr)

Repeat rounds 3 and 4 once more.

Round 8. 2ch in first st, 1tr into each of the next 7tr, decrease over next 2tr, * 1tr into each of the next 8tr, decrease over the next 2tr; repeat from * 10 more times, sl st into the top of the 2ch. (108tr)

Repeat rounds 3 and 4 once more.

Round 11. 2ch in first st, 1tr into each of the next 6tr, decrease over next 2tr, * 1tr into each of the next 7tr, decrease over the next 2tr; repeat from * 10 more times, sl st into the top of the 2ch. (96tr)

Repeat rounds 3 and 4 once more.

Round 14. 2ch in first st, 1tr into each of the next 5tr, decrease over next 2tr, * 1tr into each of the next 6tr, decrease over the next 2tr; repeat from * 10 more times, sl st into the top of the 2ch. (84tr)

Repeat rounds 3 and 4 once more.

Round 17. With right side of work facing, 1dc and 1ch in first st, 1tr in each st to end, sl st into the top of the first ch.

Round 18. Sl st across one more tr, turn work, 1ch, sl st in a row of lace, overlapping last 2 holes of lace and turning under lace to neaten edge at last st. Turn work.

Round 19. 1dc and 1ch in first st, 1tr into each of the next 4sts, decrease over next 2sts, * 1tr into each of the next 5sts, decrease over the next 2sts; repeat from * 10 more times, sl st into the top of the 1dc 1ch. (72tr)

Round 20. 2ch in first st, 1tr into each of the next 3tr, decrease over next 2tr, * 1tr into each of the next 4tr, decrease over the next 2tr; repeat from * 10 more times, sl st into the top of the 2ch. (60tr)

Repeat round 3 once only.

Round 22. 1dc and 1ch in first st, 1tr into each of the next 2sts, decrease over next 2sts, * 1tr into each of the next 3sts, decrease over the next 2sts; repeat from * 10 more times, sl st into the top of the 1dc 1ch. (48tr)

Repeat round 4 then repeat round 3.

Round 25. 1dc and 1ch in first st, 1tr into each of the next 2sts, * 2tr into the next st, 1tr into each of the next 3sts; repeat from * 10 more times, ending round with 2tr in last st. Join round with a sl st. (60tr) (This round is turned over the top of the wire frame later.) End off.

Make up: Right sides together, sew side seam taking care not to catch in the lace. Neaten edges of lace. Place over wire frame, aligning the seam over one strut. Evenly oversew top and bottom edges over the wire frame. Make 3 bows from ribbon and sew to cover. Glue flowers to bows.

6. KNITTED COMPACT TISSUE COVER

MATERIALS:
10g acrylic 8ply yarn
3.1m eyelet lace
flowers
30cm of 6mm wide ribbon
pr 4mm knitting needles

This project is knitted in garter stitch.

Cast on 18sts.

* Knit 3 rows.

Knit in a row of lace. *

Repeat from * to * 12 more times. (13 lace rows)

Knit 2 rows. Cast off loosely.

Make up: Right sides together, sew cast-on and cast-off edges together for 1.5cm at each end only (to form opening). Centralize this join and sew side seams together, taking care not to catch in the lace. Turn right side out. Trim with flowers and ribbon.

7. KNITTED LADY TOWEL MOTIF

MATERIALS:
10g 4ply cotton
hand towel
3.2m single sided eyelet lace (90 holes/m)
2.1m of 1.5mm wide ribbon
1m of 6mm wide ribbon
pr 2.5mm knitting needles

DRESS

Cast on 20sts. (Neck edge)

Rows 1 - 3. Beginning with a knit row, work in stocking stitch.

Row 4. Knit in a row of lace with lace to back and holes to bottom.

Row 5. Knit 2sts into every st. (ie. one stitch into the front of the stitch, and one stitch into the back of the stitch) (40sts)

Commencing with a purl row, work 3 rows of stocking stitch.

Row 9. Cast off 14sts, knit to end. (26sts)

Row 10. Cast off 14sts, purl to end. (12sts)

Commencing with a knit row, work 8 rows of stocking stitch.

Row 19. * Increase in first st, K1; repeat from * to end. (18sts)

Row 20. Knit in a row of lace as before.

Row 21. Knit 2sts into every st. (36sts)

Commencing with a purl row, work 8 rows of stocking stitch.

Row 30. Knit in a row of lace as before.

Row 31. * Increase in first st, K1; repeat from * to end. (54sts)

Commencing with a purl row, work 8 rows of stocking stitch.

Row 40. Knit in a row of lace as before.

Commencing with a knit row, work 9 rows of stocking stitch.

Row 50. Knit in a row of lace as before. (5 rows of lace completed)

Row 51. Knit.

Row 52. Purl. Cast off.

HAT

Cast on 10sts. (Top of hat)

Commencing with a knit row, work 4 rows of stocking stitch.

Row 5. Increase in first st, K8, increase in last st. (12sts)

Row 6. Purl.

Row 7. Increase in each of the first two sts, K8, increase in each of the last two sts. (16sts) Place marker here.

Row 8. Purl.

Row 9. Cast on 4sts. Knit to end of row, turn work and cast on another 4sts. (24sts)

Commencing with a purl row, work 4 rows of stocking stitch.

Row 14. Knit in a row of lace as before.

Row 15. Knit.

Row 16. Purl. Cast off.

Make up:
Refer to coloured picture. Thread the ribbon between the layers of lace in the skirt (row 6 of the stocking stitch), through the waist and into the eyelet holes of the lace at the neckline. Similarly, thread ribbon through eyelet holes in hat and through knitting at row 7. Stitch ends of ribbon to back of work. Sew motif to towel. Thread ribbon through remainder of eyelet lace and sew 2 rows of lace to bottom of towel. Make 4 bows from remainder of 1.5mm wide ribbon and attach to dress and hat.

8. KNITTED SCRUNCHIE

MATERIALS:
8g acrylic 8ply yarn
1.1m eyelet lace
30cm of 6mm wide elastic
pr 4mm knitting needles

This project is knitted in garter stitch.

Cast on 90sts and knit 4 rows.

Knit in a row of lace.

Knit 4 rows. Cast off loosely.

Make up:
Right sides together, join short ends of knitted strip. Join ends of elastic to form a circle. Place elastic circle to the wrong side of the knitted circle and sew together the cast-on and cast-off edges.

9. CROCHETED LADY TOWEL MOTIF

MATERIALS:
15g 4ply cotton
hand towel
3.3m single sided eyelet lace (90 holes/m)
3m of 3mm wide ribbon
2.5mm crochet hook

DRESS

Make 20ch. (Neck edge)

Row 1. 2ch, 1htr into each ch. (20htr)

Row 2. With lace to FRONT of work, holes to bottom and end folded towards you, 1ch, sl st in a row of lace. (Wrong side of work)

Row 3. 3ch, 2tr into each st behind the lace at back of work. (40tr)

Row 4. 2ch, 1htr into each st. (40htr) End off.

Row 5. Miss 15htr, join in yarn, 3ch, 1tr into each of the next 9htr. (9tr) Turn work.

Rows 6 and 7. 2ch, 1htr into each tr. (9htr)

Row 8. 2ch, 1htr into first htr, 2htr into each of the remaining htr. (17htr)

Row 9. 2ch, 1htr into each htr. (17htr)

Row 10. With lace to FRONT, 1ch, sl st in a row of lace as before.

Row 11. 2ch, 2htr into each st behind the lace. (34htr)

Rows 12 and 13. 2ch, 1htr into each htr.

Row 14. With lace to FRONT, 1ch, sl st in a row of lace as before.

Row 15. 2ch, 1htr into each st behind the lace. (34htr)

Row 16. 2ch, 1htr into first htr, * 2htr into the next htr, 1htr into next htr; repeat from * 15 more times, 1htr in last st. (50htr)

Row 17. 2ch, 1htr into each htr.

Row 18. With lace to FRONT, 1ch, sl st in a row of lace as before.

Row 19. 2ch, 1htr into each st behind the lace. (50htr)

Rows 20 and 21. 2ch, 1htr into each htr.

Row 22. With lace to FRONT, 1ch, sl st in a row of lace as before. End off.

HAT

Make 8ch. (Top of hat)

Rows 1 - 3. 2ch, 1htr into each st. (8htr)

Row 4. 2ch, 4htr into first htr, 1htr into each of the next 6htr, 4htr into the last htr. (14htr)

Row 5. 2ch, 4htr into the first htr, 1htr into each of the next 12htr, 4htr into the last htr. (20htr)

Row 6. 1ch, sl st in a row of lace to back of work but with holes to bottom. (Right side of work facing) End off.

Make up: To highlight dress and hat, thread ribbon through waist line of dress (row 6) and through each row before the lace (rows 1, 9, 13, 17 and 21) and through rows 3 and 4 of the hat. Neaten ends of ribbon to back of work. Thread ribbon through remainder of eyelet lace and sew 2 rows of lace to bottom of towel. Make bows from remainder of the ribbon and decorate as desired. Sew motif to towel.

10. KNITTED PLASTIC BAG HOLDER

MATERIALS:
55g 8ply acrylic yarn
17.5m eyelet lace
flowers to suit
2m of 15mm wide ribbon
pr 4mm knitting needles

This project is knitted in garter stitch.

Cast on 72sts. (Top of holder)

Work 3 rows of (K1, P1) rib.

* Knit in a row of lace.

Knit 5 rows. *

Repeat from * to * until 21 rows of lace have been completed.

Work 3 rows of (K1, P1) rib.

Next row. * K2 tog, P2 tog; repeat from * to end. (36sts)

Next row. Work 1 row of (K1, P1) rib. Cast off.

Make up:
Right sides together, sew centre back seam, taking care not to catch in the lace. Using 58cm of ribbon for each hanger, attach hangers at row 1, one hanger at centre back and centre front, and the other hanger at the sides. Turn right side out. Form a bow with the remainder of the ribbon. Glue flowers to the bow and sew to front of holder. (Holds about 20 plastic carry bags.)

11. KNITTED DOUBLE TOILET ROLL HOLDER

MATERIALS:
55g 8ply acrylic yarn
9m eyelet lace
75mm ring
flowers
1m of 6mm wide ribbon
pr 4mm knitting needles

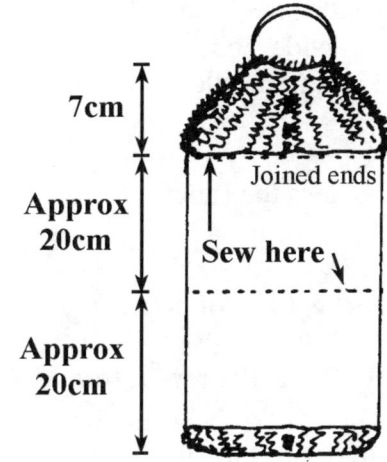

This project is knitted in garter stitch.

Cast on 28sts.

Knit 28 rows.

Row 29. * Knit in a row of lace.

Knit 5 rows. *

Repeat the last 6 rows 25 more times. (26 rows of lace completed)

Knit 113 rows.

Cast off.

Make up:
Slip ring over knitting. Right sides together, sew across narrow ends. Turn right side out. Refer diagram above. Position joined ends to the back and 7cm down as shown. Sew through all thicknesses at joined ends and middle of hanger. Decorate with flowers and bows.

12. KNITTED BOOTEES

Size: 8.5cm underfoot seam

MATERIALS:
20g 4ply cotton (or 3ply wool)
4m fine single sided eyelet lace (100 holes/m)
1m of 6mm wide ribbon
pr 3mm knitting needles

Make 2 bootees the same.

Cast on 38sts. (Top of bootee)

** **Row 1.** * K1, P1; repeat from * to end of row. (rib)

Work 4 more rows of rib.

Row 6. Knit in a row of lace, with frilled edge to top. **

Repeat last 6 rows twice more. (3 rows of lace completed)

Rows 19 and 20. Rib.

Row 21. K1, * yarn forward, K2 tog; repeat from * to last stitch, K1.

Row 22. Rib. (17 ribbon holes made)

INSTEP (worked in stocking stitch)

Row 1. K25, push the remaining 13sts to one end of the needle and work on these 25sts only.

Row 2. P12, push the remaining 13sts to one end and work on these 12sts.

Beginning with a knit row, work 17 rows of stocking st, turn work.

The remainder of this project is knitted in garter stitch.

Row 20. Wrong side of work facing, cast on 14sts. Now knit these 14sts, knit the 12 instep stitches, turn work, cast on 14sts, cut yarn and push the other 13sts onto the needle. *Wrong side of work facing*, rejoin yarn. (66sts)

Next Row. Knit in a row of lace.

Work 10 rows in garter stitch.

FOOT *Shape foot as follows:*

Row 1. (Right side) K5, K2 tog, K18, K2 tog, K12, K2 tog, K18, K2 tog, K5. (62sts)

Row 2. Knit.

Row 3. K4, K2 tog, K18, K2 tog, K10, K2 tog, K18, K2 tog, K4. (58sts)

Row 4. Knit.

Row 5. K3, K2 tog, K18, K2 tog, K8, K2 tog, K18, K2 tog, K3. (54sts)

Row 6. Knit.

Row 7. K2, K2 tog, K18, K2 tog, K6, K2 tog, K18, K2 tog, K2. (50sts)

Row 8. Knit.

Row 9. K1, K2 tog, K18, K2 tog, K4, K2 tog, K18, K2 tog, K1. (46sts) Cast off.

Make up:
Right sides together, sew instep seams, centre back seam and underfoot seam. Turn right side out. Thread half the ribbon through the ribbon holes and tie in a bow at front.

13. CROCHETED BOOTEES

Size: 8cm underfoot seam

MATERIALS:
4ply cotton or 3ply wool
4m fine single sided eyelet lace (100 holes/m)
1m of 6mm wide ribbon
2.5mm crochet hook

Make 2 bootees the same.

Using a 2.5mm crochet hook make 30ch. (Top of bootee)

Rows 1 and 2. 2ch, 1htr into each st. (30htr)

Row 3. 1ch, sl st in a row of lace, with lace to back of work and frill to top.

** **Row 4.** 2ch, 1tr in each st to end. (30tr)

Row 5. 1ch, sl st in a row of lace. **

Repeat last 2 rows twice more. (4 rows of lace completed)

Row 10. 2ch, 1htr in each st. (30htr)

Row 11. 2ch, 1htr in first htr, * miss 1htr, 1ch, 1htr in next htr; repeat from * to last st, 1htr in last st. (14 ribbon holes)

Row 12. Cut thread, and with right side of work uppermost, miss 11sts, join in yarn and work 8htr over the next 8sts. These stitches will begin the instep. Turn work.

Work another 6 rows of htr on these 8sts. (8htr)

Cut thread. With right side of work uppermost, rejoin yarn at right hand side of ribbon holes.

Row 19. Work 11dc over the htr and 1ch spaces previously missed, 11dc up the side of the instep, 8dc over front of instep, 11dc down the other side of the instep, and 11dc over the other htr and 1ch spaces. (52dc)

Row 20. 1ch, sl st in a row of lace. (5 rows of lace completed)

Work 3 rows of htr on these 52sts.

Row 24. 2ch, 1htr in each of the first 5htr, decrease over next 2htr, 1htr in each of the next 13htr, decrease over the next 2htr, 1htr in each of the next 8htr, decrease over the next 2htr, 1htr in each of the next 13htr, decrease over the next 2htr, 1htr in each of the next 5htr. (48htr)

Row 25. 2ch, 1htr in each of the first 4htr, decrease over next 2htr, 1htr in each of the next 13htr, decrease over the next 2htr, 1htr in each of the next 6htr, decrease over the next 2htr, 1htr in each of the next 13htr, decrease over the next 2htr, 1htr in each of the next 4htr. (44htr)

Row 26. 2ch, 1htr in each of the first 3htr, decrease over next 2htr, 1htr in each of the next 13htr, decrease over the next 2htr, 1htr in each of the next 4htr, decrease over the next 2htr, 1htr in each of the next 13htr, decrease over the next 2htr, 1htr in each of the next 3htr. (40htr)

Row 27. 2ch, 1htr in each of the first 2htr, decrease over next 2htr, 1htr in each of the next 13htr, decrease over the next 2htr, 1htr in each of the next 2htr, decrease over the next 2htr, 1htr in each of the next 13htr, decrease over the next 2htr, 1htr in each of the next 2htr. (36htr)

Make up:

Right sides together, sew instep seams, centre back seam and underfoot seam. Turn right side out. Thread half the ribbon through the ribbon holes and tie in a bow at front.

14. KNITTED TISSUE BOX COVER

This pattern fits 100 - 125 size. For larger boxes, add more rows of fancy eyelet lace. Each row requires 95cm of fancy single sided gathered eyelet lace.

MATERIALS:
30g 8ply yarn
5.1m double sided eyelet lace
2.8m (357 holes) of 3.5cm wide single sided gathered eyelet lace (130 holes/m)
flowers
40cm of 6mm wide ribbon
pr each of 3.25mm and 4mm knitting needles

This project is knitted in garter stitch.

TOP OF BOX COVER

Using 4mm needles, cast on 37sts, and knit 1 row.

Row 2. Knit in a row of double sided eyelet lace.

** Knit 3 rows.

Knit in a row of double sided eyelet lace. **

Repeat last 4 rows three more times. (5 rows of lace completed)

Row 19. Knit.

Row 20. K11, turn work. Work on these 11sts only.

Row 21. Knit. (11sts)

Row 22. Knit in a row of double sided eyelet lace.

Knit 2 rows, then cut thread and push stitches to one end of needle.

Turn work, (wrong side facing) join in yarn and cast off 15sts, knit to end of row. (11sts)

Next row. Knit.

Next row. Knit in a row of double sided eyelet lace.

Knit 3 rows.

Turn work and cast on 15sts, turn work, knit other 11sts (pushed to end of needle previously). (37sts) Opening completed.

** **Next row.** Knit in a row of lace.

Knit 3 rows. **

Repeat last 4 rows 4 more times. (5 rows of lace completed for second half of top)

SIDE OF BOX COVER

With right side of work uppermost, cast on 77sts, placing markers at the 20th and 57th cast-on stitch. These are the corners. (114sts)

Row 1. Knit.

Row 2. With frill to top and wrong side of lace facing, knit in a row of wide fancy lace.

Knit 7 rows.

Repeat last 8 rows once more, then row 2. (3 rows of lace completed)

Change to 3.25mm needles and knit 12 rows. Cast off.

Make up:
Right sides together, join side seam. Using the markers as references for the corners, sew top of box cover to sides. Decorate with ribbon and flowers.

15. KNITTED GOLF CLUB COVER

MATERIALS:
20g 8ply acrylic yarn
3.4m eyelet lace
pr each 3.25mm and 4mm knitting needles.

Using 3.25mm needles cast on 42sts.

Row 1. * K1, P1; repeat from * to end of row. (rib)

Work another 53 rows of rib. (16cm)

Row 55. K2, * increase in next st, K3; repeat from * 9 more times. (52sts)

Change to 4mm needles. The remainder of the project is knitted in garter st.

** Knit 3 rows.

Knit in a row of lace. **

Repeat last 4 rows four more times. (5 rows of lace completed)

Row 76. Knit. (52sts)

Row 77. * K2, K2 tog; repeat from * to end. (39sts)

Row 78. * K1, K2 tog; repeat from * to end. (26sts)

Row 79. Knit in a row of lace.

Row 80. Knit.

Row 81. * K2 tog; repeat from * to end. (13sts) Thread the yarn through these stitches and secure.

Make up: Right sides together, sew up side seam. Turn right side out.

16. CROCHETED TIDY BAG

MATERIALS:
125g 4ply cotton
7.2m double sided eyelet lace
wire coat hanger
20cm of wadding
4mm plastic tubing for hanger
plastic coat hanger tip
flowers
4.5m of 3mm wide ribbon
50cm of 15mm wide ribbon
3.5mm crochet hook

BACK OF HANGER

Make 61ch.

Rows 1 - 3. 2ch, 1htr in each st. (61htr)

Row 4. 2ch, decrease over next 2htr, 1htr in each htr to last 2sts, decrease over next 2sts. (59htr)

Repeat row 4 twelve more times. (35htr)

Row 17. 2ch, (decrease over next 2sts) twice, 1htr in each htr to last 4sts, (decrease over next 2sts) twice. (31htr)

Repeat row 17 six more times. (7htr)

Row 24. 2ch, decrease over first 2sts, 1htr in each of the next 3sts, decrease over the next 2sts. (5htr)

Row 25. 2ch, decrease over first 2sts, 1htr in next st, decrease over the last 2sts. (3htr) End off.

FRONT OF HANGER

Make 61ch.

Row 1. 2ch, 1htr in each st. (61htr)

Row 2. 1ch, sl st in a row of lace.

Work 2 rows of htr.

Row 5. 2ch, decrease over next 2htr, 1htr in each htr to last 2sts, decrease over next 2sts. (59htr)

Row 6. 1ch, sl st in a row of lace.

** Repeat row 5 three more times. (53htr)

Row 10. 1ch, sl st in a row of lace. **

Repeat from ** to ** 3 more times. (35htr and 6 rows of lace completed)

Rows 23 - 25. 2ch, (decrease over next 2sts) twice, 1htr in each htr to last 4sts, (decrease over next 2sts) twice. (23htr)

Row 26. 1ch, sl st in a row of lace.

Repeat row 23 three more times. (11htr)

Row 30. 1ch, sl st in a row of lace. (8 rows of lace)

Row 31. As per row 23. (7htr)

Row 32. 2ch, decrease over first 2sts, 1htr in each of the next 3sts, decrease over the last 2sts. (5htr)

Row 33. 2ch, decrease over first 2sts, 1htr in next st, decrease over the last 2sts. (3htr) End off.

BOTTOM OF TIDY BAG

Make 60ch.

Rows 1 - 3. 2ch, 1htr in each st. (60htr)

Row 4. 1ch, sl st in a row of lace.

Work 5 rows of htr.

Row 10. 1ch, sl st in a row of lace.

Repeat last 6 rows once more. (3 rows of lace completed)

Work 89 rows of htr.

** **Row 106.** 1ch, sl st in a row of lace.

Work 5 rows of htr. **

Repeat last 6 rows once more.

Row 118. 1ch, sl st in a row of lace. (6 rows of lace)

Work 3 rows of htr. End off.

Make up:
Pad coat hanger with wadding. Right sides together, join back and front of hanger pieces leaving the bottom edge open.

Refer to coloured picture. Thread the ribbon between the lace rows of the tidy bag. Also thread the ribbon into the 4th, 8th and 12th rows out from the lace rows for 17cm, 14cm and 9cm respectively. Sew folded ends of ribbon into place.

Right sides together, join first and last rows of tidy bag for 1cm at top and 14cm at bottom. Work a row of dc around this opening. Centralize this opening and sew across the bottom of the bag.

Right sides together join tidy bag to hanger making sure that the central opening of tidy bag lines up with the centre of the lace hanger. Insert padded hanger, poking hole through the top of the hanger pieces. Sew crocheting to top of hanger. Make bows from the remainder of the 3mm wide ribbon and decorate bag. Thread plastic tubing over hanger wire and add plastic tip. Decorate the top of hanger with flowers and the 15mm wide ribbon

17. CROCHETED WIRE COAT HANGER COVER

MATERIALS:
30g of 4ply cotton
8.3m double sided eyelet lace
wire coat hanger
20cm wadding
4mm plastic tubing for hanger
plastic coat hanger tip
flowers
40cm of 10mm wide ribbon
3.5mm crochet hook

Front and **back** alike. Make 2.

Work as for the *FRONT OF HANGER* of **CROCHETED TIDY BAG** on page 30.

Make up:
Pad coat hanger with wadding. Right sides together, join back and front pieces, leaving the bottom edge open. Turn right side out. Insert wire coat hanger. The crocheting will need to stretch a little. Oversew bottom edge. Sew crocheting to top of hanger. Push 4mm plastic tubing over wire hanger and finish with a plastic tip. Decorate with ribbon and flowers.

18. KNITTED ANGEL

MATERIALS:
8ply yarn
5.5m eyelet lace
small doll 20cm high
pr of 9cm long angel wings
2 contrasting 6mm glitter chenille stems
60cm of 3mm wide ribbon
45cm of 6mm wide ribbon
2 small Christmas decorations
polystyrene take away cup
pr 4mm knitting needles

This project is knitted in garter stitch

Cast on 55sts and knit 2 rows.

Row 3. Knit in a row of lace.

Knit 3 rows.

Row 7. Knit in a row of lace.

Knit 2 rows.

Row 10. * K9, K2 tog; repeat from * to end. (50sts)

Row 11. Knit in a row of lace.

Knit 2 rows.

Row 14. * K8, K2 tog; repeat from * to end. (45sts)

Row 15. Knit in a row of lace.

Knit 2 rows.

Row 18. * K7, K2 tog; repeat from * to end. (40sts)

Row 19. Knit in a row of lace.

Knit 2 rows.

Row 22. * K6, K2 tog; repeat from * to end. (35sts)

Row 23. Knit in a row of lace.

Knit 2 rows.

Row 26. * K5, K2 tog; repeat from * to end. (30sts)

Row 27. Knit in a row of lace.

Knit 2 rows.

Row 30. * K4, K2 tog; repeat from * to end. (25sts)

Row 31. Knit in a row of lace. (8 rows of lace completed)

Knit 3 rows.

Knit in a row of lace.

Repeat last 4 rows once more.

Row 40. Knit.

Row 41. K6, K2 tog, K9, K2 tog, K6. (23sts)

Row 42. K6, increase over next st, K9, increase over next st, K6. (25sts) (Armholes made)

Row 43. Knit in a row of lace.

Knit 3 rows.

Row 47. Knit in a row of lace. (12 rows of lace completed)

Make up: Draw up yarn through remainder of stitches. Right sides together, and starting at bottom of the skirt, sew up centre back seam to waist. Turn right side out. Place on doll and sew remainder of seam, tying off the neck stitches with this yarn.

Make a halo from 10cm of each colour of chenille stem by twisting them together. Glue halo to hair. Glue and pin wings to back of doll, inserting the pins into the doll. Tie a bow from the 6mm wide ribbon and glue over the centre of the wings.

Tie a small decoration to the doll's arm with the 3mm wide ribbon and finish with a bow. Glue the other decoration and a bow from the remainder of the ribbon to the front of the dress.

Cut a small hole in the base of the polystyrene cup so that the doll's legs can be inserted. Push the doll through the hole so that the cup forms a petticoat and allows the doll to stand by herself. This can be used as a tree decoration or a table centre piece.

BK01	Katrina's Christmas Earrings
BK02	Hooked on Lace
BK03	Needles and Lace
BK04	Top that Towel
BK05	Laced with Love
BK06	More Towel Tops
BK07	Novelties in Lace
BK08	Paragon of Lace
BK09	Keep it Cosy
BK10	Basics in Lace
BK11	Knitted Coat-hanger Covers
BK12	Towel Tops & Motifs
BK13	Simple Jug Covers
BK14	More Knitted Lace
BK15	Easy Crocheted Bootees
BK16	Kitchen Towels
BK17	Doilies for my Daughter
BK18	Baby's Crocheted Rugs and Shawls
BK19	Crocheted Matinee Jackets
BK20	Baby's Knitted Rugs and Shawls
BK21	More Jug Covers
BK22	Crocheted Three Piece Sets
BKAG01	Sculptured Candlewicking (by Anne Green)
BKAG02	Australiana Candlewicking (by Anne Green)
BKAG03	Country Applique and Candlewicking (by Green & Jellicoe)

PARAGON BOOKS

CROCHET BOOKS (PARC series)

PARCR2   **A COLLECTION OF EVER POPULAR DOILIES.** 15 crochet patterns for round doilies from 11 - 46cm diameters using No 40 and 60 crochet cotton.

PARC102   **PINEAPPLE CROCHET DESIGNS.** 13 crochet patterns for dressing table set and doilies from 15 - 57cm diameters, table runner, tablecloths and bedspreads using No 20 and 40 crochet cotton.

PARC103   **CROCHET EDGINGS.** Patterns for 46 crocheted edges using No 20, 40 and 60 crochet cotton.

PARC104   **LEARN TO TAT.** Learn to tat instructions and patterns for dressing table sets and 14 edges using No 20, 40 and 60 crochet cotton.

PARC106   **CROCHET DESIGNS.** 9 crochet patterns for mats, cloths and doilies using No 5 to 60 cotton.

PARC108   **ATTRACTIVE DOILIES.** 8 patterns for 3 piece set and doilies from 20 - 56cm diameters using No 10, 20 and 40 crochet cotton.

PARC109   **EVERY PURPOSE CROCHET MOTIFS.** 21 motifs for doilies to bedspreads using No 20 to 60 crochet cotton.

PARC111   **CROCHET EDGES.** 11 crochet edges for mats, cloths, handkerchiefs, church lace and altar cloth using No 20, 40 and 60 crochet cotton.

PARC122   **CROCHETED FLORAL DOILIES.** 6 doily designs in No 20 crochet cotton; includes butterfly, water-lily and rose doilies and pansy luncheon set.

PARC126   **LEARN TO CROCHET.** Illustrated instructions of basic techniques and stitches for left and right handers with easy patterns for doilies and edges.

PARC129   **SIX CROCHETED DOILIES.** 6 crocheted doilies in No 20 crochet cotton from 28 - 48cm diameters; includes oval mat with wheat design, round pinecone doily and a large doily, which can be beaded.

KNITTING BOOKS (PARK series)

PARK03   **EXCLUSIVE KNITWEAR FOR BABY.** Includes 9-piece layette, jackets and 12 pr bootees in 3ply yarn.

PARK24   **7 STYLES 2 TO 5 YEARS.** 7 knitted jumpers/cardigans in 3, 4 and 8ply yarn for children 2 to 5 years.

PARK31   **BONNETS BOOTEES AND MITTENS.** Knitted patterns in 3ply yarn for babies from birth to 12 months.

PARK38   **THE SOCK BOOK.** 11 knitted adjustable sized socks in 3 and 4ply yarn from toddlers to adults.

PARK60   **YEAR ROUND BOOTEES.** 12 pr of adjustable sized bootees, 2 matching sets of bonnets, bootees and mittens and a jacket to suit a 45 - 50cm chest, using 3 and 4ply yarn.

PARK66   **CUDDLE CARDIGANS.** 10 knitted cardigans in 3 and 4ply yarn suit from birth to 2 years.

PARK207   **BOOTEE BOOK.** 21 pr of baby bootees, each pr in 3 sizes birth to 9 months, all using 3ply yarn.

PARK208   **BONNETS AND HELMETS.** 13 knitting patterns using 3 and 4ply yarn for bonnets, helmets and berets for babies from birth to 12 months.

PARK601   **BAZAAR AND GIFT BOOK.** 16 knitted projects for fetes and gifts; includes toys, tea cosies, doll's layette, hot-water bottle cover, shopping bag, bed socks, cushion cover and a golliwog.

PARK633   **QUICKLY KNITTED CLOTHES FOR DOLLS.** 6 complete outfits in 8ply yarn, all to suit dolls 30, 35 and 40cm high and one outfit for a doll 51cm high.

PARK643   **THE TOY BOX.** A delightful collection of 10 lovable, simple to make, quickly knitted toys all in 8ply yarn.

PARK656   **DOLL'S CLOTHES IN DOUBLE KNITTING.** 23 outfits in 8ply yarn to suit baby, little girl and teenage style dolls from 25 to 50cm high.